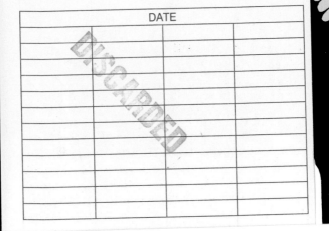

DISCARDED

Wright, Rachel.

Plundering pirates.

$3.99   02/08/2002

DATE		

CAMBRIDGE, MASSACHUSETTS

WHEN PIRATES RULED THE WAVES

Pirates are thieves who rob ships at sea. Pirates have been around for a very long time, and some still exist today. However, the dreadful doings you're about to discover happened mainly in the 17th and 18th centuries. Back then, if there was a ship with goods worth stealing, you could be sure that pirates were never far away!

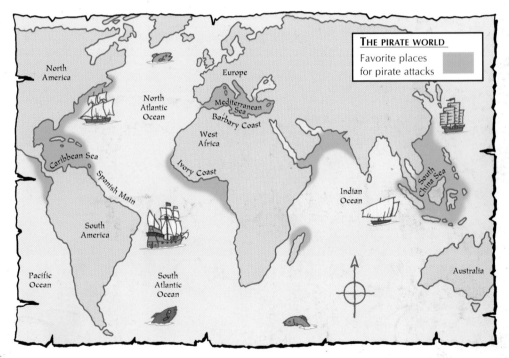

Did you know that there were different kinds of pirates? Buccaneers were pirates who hid out and raided ships in the Caribbean. Corsairs lurked in the Mediterranean Sea. Privateers had their country's permission to raid enemy trading ships. So now you know!

SHIPS OF PREY

Anchors aweigh! Our four fact-finding friends have just stepped onboard a ship in the cutthroat Caribbean Sea. Pirates didn't have special ships made just for plundering. Usually they used whatever ships they captured. Many pirates preferred a speedy ship like this 18th-century schooner, because it was perfect for sneaking up on prey and then making a quick getaway.

The huge rudder could be moved left or right to steer the ship.

The keel is the low **timber** of a wo͟ ͟ailing ship. Man͟ ͟ ͟s liked ships whose ke͟ ͟idn't sink low in the water so they could sail into shallow creeks and bays.

SHIP SHAPES

Pirates in different parts of the world used different types of ships, whatever was most common to the region.

Galley: Corsairs on the Mediterranean Sea did their plundering in ships with oars, called galleys. The galleys were rowed by slaves, who were chained to benches below deck.

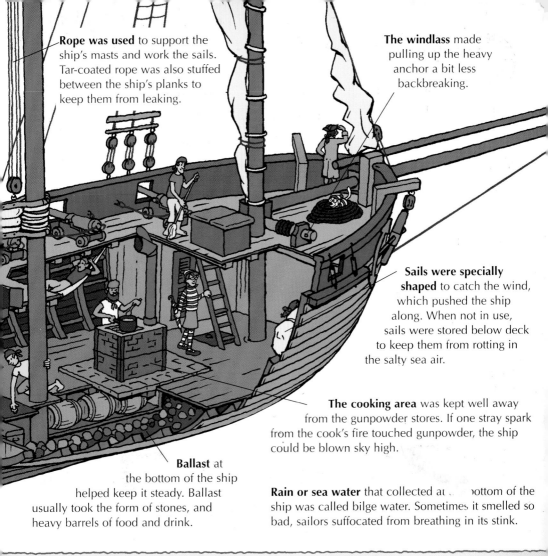

Rope was used to support the ship's masts and work the sails. Tar-coated rope was also stuffed between the ship's planks to keep them from leaking.

The windlass made pulling up the heavy anchor a bit less backbreaking.

Sails were specially shaped to catch the wind, which pushed the ship along. When not in use, sails were stored below deck to keep them from rotting in the salty sea air.

The cooking area was kept well away from the gunpowder stores. If one stray spark from the cook's fire touched gunpowder, the ship could be blown sky high.

Ballast at the bottom of the ship helped keep it steady. Ballast usually took the form of stones, and heavy barrels of food and drink.

Rain or sea water that collected at the bottom of the ship was called bilge water. Sometimes it smelled so bad, sailors suffocated from breathing in its stink.

Junk: *Chinese pirates sailed local boats called junks. When they captured a trading junk, they added cannons to make it more warlike.*

Two-masted schooner: *Pirates in the North Atlantic Ocean and the Caribbean Sea often used schooners that could carry crews of 75 men.*

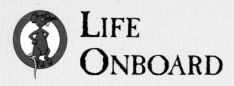

LIFE ONBOARD

The inside of a sailing ship was dark and damp, and on long voyages the food was often terrible. Sailors didn't have refrigerators, so meat and fish were smothered in salt to keep them from spoiling. Instead of bread, which soon goes stale, sailors ate hardtack biscuits made from flour and water. Packed in cloth bags, these became infested with weevils. Imagine biting into a biscuit full of bugs!

~ MENU ~

Salty meat
and crawly biscuits
~
Crawly biscuits
and salty meat
~
Rat-atoowee
(without the -atoowee)
~
Spirits

To help save space, the crew slept in foldaway hammocks or on the deck.

Like other ships in the 17th and 18th centuries, pirate ships often kept hens for their eggs.

When they weren't busy plundering, or repairing their ship, pirates sometimes relaxed by playing cards and dice.

A pirate who could play a musical instrument was popular onboard because crews liked to sing and dance to pass the time.

Without fresh food and clean drinking water, sailors often got sick. Because living quarters below deck were so cramped, disease spread quickly.

Hardtack was sometimes so hard, you could carve your name into it.

Ships were plagued by cockroaches, bugs, and rats. Rats were a real pest because they chomped their way through everything, including wood and rope.

GREETINGS, BOOK-WORMS! DID YOU KNOW THAT PIRATES AND OTHER SAILORS COLLECTED PARROTS AS SOUVENIRS? THEY EVEN ENJOYED TEACHING THE BIRDS TO SPEAK. FANTASTIC! CAN YOU SPY A COLORFUL PARROT SOMEWHERE ON THIS SHIP?

BEHAVE, OR ELSE!

Each pirate ship had its own set of rules that all crew had to obey. One common rule was: No women onboard ship. Let's hope nobody discovers Wenda's flimsy disguise!

RULES FOR BARTHOLOMEW ROBERTS'S CREW

OBEY, OR ELSE!

- Any man who robs another will have his ears and nose slit and will be put ashore.

- Any man who runs away from a battle will be killed or marooned (left alone on a deserted island).

- No gambling for money with dice or cards.

- Each man must keep his weapons clean and ready for action.

- Ship's musicians may have a day off on Sunday only.

- Lights and candles out by 8 P.M., sharp!

- No hitting each other onboard ship.

- All quarrels must be settled on shore with a sword or pistol.

- All big decisions must be put to the vote.

- Any man who has lost an arm or a leg in battle will be given extra plunder.

PAINFUL PUNISHMENT

For pirates and other sailors who disobeyed ship rules, dreadful discipline was in store. The most common punishment was whipping, or flogging, with a rope.

LONELY DEATH

Being flogged wasn't fun . . . but it was better than being marooned. Marooned pirates were left on a deserted island with only a bottle of water and a gun. Few were ever picked up by a passing ship.

FAIR'S FAIR

Life on a pirate ship was often fairer than life onboard navy and trading ships. In fact, some sailors became pirates to escape the unfair punishments of cruel navy officers. Unlike ordinary ships' captains, a pirate captain gave orders only in battle. At other times, important decisions were put to a vote.

Pirates who committed minor crimes were punished by the ship's quartermaster, who was the second-in-command. Serious troublemakers were judged by the whole crew.

GUESS WHAT, FELLOW FACT-FINDERS! THERE'S LITTLE PROOF THAT "WALKING THE PLANK" WAS AN ACTUAL PIRATE PUNISHMENT. INCREDIBLE!

LAND AHOY!

Pirates didn't spend all day every day sailing the seven seas. They popped into ports frequently to spend their money and to stock up on fresh food and water. They often beached their ship in hidden bays so that they could clean and repair the outside, or hull. Barnacles and weeds had to be burned off regularly, because, if left there to grow for too long, they slowed down the ship.

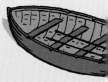

LANDLUBBERS

People who worked on land and knew nothing about ships were nicknamed "landlubbers" by sailors. The only landlubbers pirates had any use for were surgeons and musicians. But how many pirates do you think would have wanted "Surgeon" Odlaw onboard?

HEAVY CLEANING

Cleaning a ship's hull was hard work. First, the ship was tipped on its side so that the crew could clean the exposed side and replace any damaged planks. Then it was refloated, turned around, and tipped onto its other side so that the rest of the hull could be cleaned and repaired.

PORT ROYAL ON THE ISLAND OF JAMAICA WAS ONCE A HOT SPOT FOR PIRATES. THE GOVERNORS OF JAMAICA WELCOMED PIRATES TO THE ISLAND BECAUSE THEY BELIEVED THEY SCARED OFF FOREIGN INVADERS. IN 1692, PORT ROYAL SUFFERED A TERRIBLE BLOW. IT WAS HIT BY AN EARTHQUAKE, THEN FLOODED BY A TIDAL WAVE. MUCH OF THE TOWN WAS LOST BENEATH THE SEA.

PIRATE ATTACK!

Popping pistols! Odlaw's got himself mixed up in a pirate attack! Pirates often used trickery on their victims. One popular ploy was to fly the flag of a friendly country, and sail up to the victims' vessel. Once close enough, the pirates took down the friendly flag, threw grappling hooks attached to ropes onto the deck to pull the two ships together, and leaped aboard. The crew of the captured ship was usually so surprised by the attack, it had little choice but to surrender without a fight.

A PIRATE LOOKOUT KEPT WATCH FROM THE "CROW'S NEST," ATOP A MAST. HE USED A TELESCOPE TO SEE IF A SHIP WAS WORTH ROBBING OR IF IT WAS A NAVY PIRATE-BUSTING VESSEL BEST AVOIDED. CAN YOU FIND THE HIDDEN TELESCOPE IN THIS SCENE?

WICKED WEAPONS

No pirate worth his salt would have entered a fight without some trusty weapons in hand.

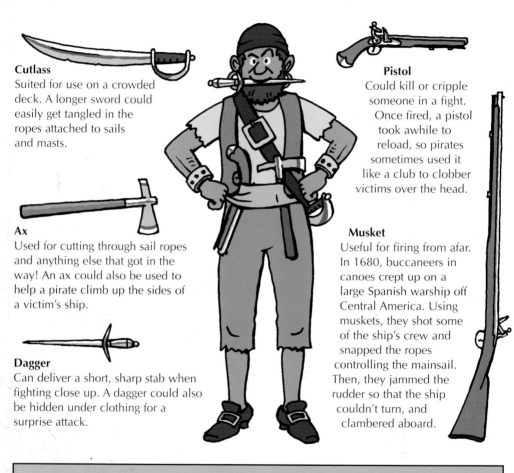

Cutlass
Suited for use on a crowded deck. A longer sword could easily get tangled in the ropes attached to sails and masts.

Ax
Used for cutting through sail ropes and anything else that got in the way! An ax could also be used to help a pirate climb up the sides of a victim's ship.

Dagger
Can deliver a short, sharp stab when fighting close up. A dagger could also be hidden under clothing for a surprise attack.

Pistol
Could kill or cripple someone in a fight. Once fired, a pistol took awhile to reload, so pirates sometimes used it like a club to clobber victims over the head.

Musket
Useful for firing from afar. In 1680, buccaneers in canoes crept up on a large Spanish warship off Central America. Using muskets, they shot some of the ship's crew and snapped the ropes controlling the mainsail. Then, they jammed the rudder so that the ship couldn't turn, and clambered aboard.

Pirates from Southeast Asia used local weaponry, like spears and blowpipes. The arrows that fired out of a blowpipe were poison tipped, to make them even deadlier.

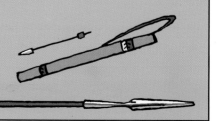

SHOT TALK!

When pirates fired a cannonball across the front of another ship, it meant "Surrender, or else!" When they snapped another ship's mast with a well-aimed shot, it left the ship unable to sail away.

CANNONS FOR BEGINNERS

Firing a cannon wasn't the speediest of jobs. Here's what a gun crew-member had to do:

1 Load cartridge of gunpowder into cannon.

2 Ram some old rope in behind the cartridge with a ramrod.

3 Load cannonball or other kind of shot and ram in more old rope.

4 Pierce gunpowder cartridge with thin piece of pointed iron. Pour more gunpowder down the hole.

5 Attach lighted wick to end of ramrod and hold to hole until a spark lights the gunpowder.

6 Block ears and stand clear!

BOOM!

RUNAWAY GUNS

The force of firing was so powerful, cannons had to be tied in place with ropes. Sometimes a cannon recoiled so violently, its ropes snapped, leaving it to roll dangerously around the gun deck. Mind your toes, Woof!

LOADS OF LOOT

Pirate crews liked their plunder to be divided fairly. On Captain Bartholomew Roberts's ship, both he and his quartermaster each received two shares of stolen treasure. Ordinary crew members got one share each. Any man caught taking more than his fair share risked being marooned. Odlaw, you have been warned!

USEFUL TREASURE

Capturing a ship loaded with money was every pirate's dream because coins, like pieces of eight, were valuable and could be divided easily. Useful things, like food, rope, weapons, and medicines, were popular plunder, too.

PEOPLE PLUNDER

Wealthy passengers from captured ships were sometimes held for ransom. Ordinary people were often killed, set adrift in a boat, or sold as slaves. Many pirates came from the crews of captured ships. Some leaped at the chance of becoming pirates. Others needed a bit of persuading!

BORING BOOTY

Sometimes pirates captured things they didn't really need, like silks, linen, or velvet. These they would sell or swap at markets on shore. In 1724, John Gow's crew captured a ship off Newfoundland only to find it was packed with fish. After stealing the anchors, ropes, and sails, they sank the ship, fish and all.

BELIEVE IT OR NOT, PIRATES DIDN'T ALWAYS BURY THEIR TREASURE! IN FACT, MANY SPENT WHAT THEY STOLE AS FAST AS THEY COULD. ONE PIRATE WHO DID BURY TREASURE WAS CAPTAIN KIDD. IT WAS PROBABLY SOME OF HIS FORTUNE THAT WAS FOUND ON GARDINER'S ISLAND OFF NEW YORK IN 1699. SPEAKING OF TREASURE, CAN YOU FIND WHERE WOOF HAS LEFT HIS MUCH-TREASURED BONE?

Fearsome Flags

Shiver-me-timbers! Our four friends have just seen the dreaded Jolly Roger loom into view. When pirates flew the Jolly Roger, it was a warning to their victims to give up without a fight. If they flew a red flag instead, it meant that they intended to fight until all victims were dead. No wonder honest seamen went wobbly at the knees whenever they saw either flag!

GUESS WHAT, FLAG-FOLLOWERS? THE FIRST PIRATE FLAGS WERE RED, AND THE NAME JOLLY ROGER PROBABLY COMES FROM THE FRENCH WORDS FOR PRETTY RED – JOLIE ROUGE. AS FOR ODLAW'S FLAG, LEAVE IT TO HIM TO DECORATE IT WITH LOOT!

DEADLY DESIGNS

The Jolly Roger, or pirate flag, didn't always have a skull and crossbones on it. In fact, many pirate captains designed their own flags.

Henry Avery's flag

The skull and crossbones was a well-known sign of death.

Christopher Moody's flag

An hourglass told pirates' victims that their time on Earth was running out.

Bartholomew Roberts's flag

Like swords and bones, skeletons were popular on pirate flags.

Blackbeard's flag

A devil-like skeleton stabbing a bleeding heart must have made victims panic!

STICKY ENDS

For pirates who were caught by the law, a nasty end was in store! A common punishment for those found guilty of piracy was death by hanging. The convicted pirate was allowed, if he wished, to make a speech to the crowd who came to watch him hang. After the execution, his speech was often printed.

BLACKBEARD CLOBBERED

Not all pirates were captured alive! In 1718, a navy lieutenant called Robert Maynard ambushed a pirate crew led by Captain Blackbeard. In the fight, Blackbeard was wounded 25 times before falling down dead.

MAN OVERBOARD

In 1722, Bartholomew Roberts and his crew

were chased by a huge British navy ship called *Swallow*. Everyone knew that *Swallow* could outgun any pirate ship. Nevertheless, Roberts ordered his crew to fight back . . . and was shot in the neck and killed. His body was then thrown overboard by his crew, as he had requested.

FULL STEAM AHEAD

The last pirate sentenced to death in England was executed in 1840. The last pirate execution in the U.S.A. took place in 1862. By this time the British and U.S. navies had steamships, so pirates didn't stand much of a chance.

VILE VILLAINS

If ever you've wanted to meet a famous pirate, here's your chance!

William Kidd
Defended English ships from pirates before he became a pirate himself! In 1701 he was hanged for piracy and murder.

The Barbarossa Brothers
From 1500 to 1546, this pair of Muslim corsairs ruled piracy in the Mediterranean Sea. They terrorized Christian ships and coastal towns, and built up a strong following of Muslim fans.

WILLIAM KIDD

THE BARBAROSSA BROTHERS

Blackbeard

The most fearsome-looking pirate ever to sail the seas, he went into battle with smoking wicks tucked into his hat. He died horribly in 1718.

Bartholomew Roberts

Roberts was probably the most successful pirate of all. Between 1720 and 1722, he is said to have captured 400 ships.

Ching Shih

One of China's most famous sea robbers. At the height of her power, she ruled a pirate fleet of about 1,800 junks and smaller boats. Her cutthroat career came to an end in 1810, when she was forced to surrender to the law.

BLACKBEARD

BARTHOLOMEW ROBERTS

CHING SHIH

THE PLUNDERING PIRATES CHECKLISTS

CALLING ALL WHERE'S WALDO? TIME-TRAVELERS! NOW THAT YOU CAN TELL A POPPING PISTOL FROM A MIGHTY MUSKET, SAIL BACK TO THE BEGINNING OF THE BOOK AND START SEARCHING FOR ALL THESE PIRATICAL THINGS.

PIRATES CHECKLIST

- [ ] Seven swimming sharks
- [ ] Eleven pesky rats
- [ ] A message in a bottle
- [ ] A pirate with a peg leg (twice)
- [ ] Six skulls and crossbones
- [ ] A treasure chest key
- [ ] Two brightly colored books
- [ ] A rolled scroll
- [ ] Three pirates wearing eyepatches
- [ ] A yellow bandanna with purple dots
- [ ] Two deserted dice
- [ ] Eight anchors
- [ ] Twenty-five real swords
- [ ] Twenty-five powerful pistols
- [ ] Four mighty muskets

DOUBLE VISION

Can you remember where you first spied these buccaneering bits and pieces?

WHO'S A PRETTY BOY, THEN?

All these faces appear in the book, but not exactly as they look here. Can you spot the differences?

ANSWERS

Life Onboard — The parrot sits on the purple pirate's shoulder.
Pirate Attack! — The spyglass lies by the cannon's wheel.
Loads of Loot — Woof's bone is behind a golden goblet.

Copyright © 2000 by Martin Handford
All rights reserved.
First U.S. edition 2001
Library of Congress Cataloging-in-Publication Data
is available.
Library of Congress Catalog Card Number 00-023144
ISBN 0-7636-1300-2
1 2 3 4 5 6 7 8 9 10
This book was typeset in Optima.
The illustrations were done in ink
and colored electronically.
Printed in Hong Kong
Candlewick Press
2067 Massachusetts Avenue
Cambridge, Massachusetts 02140